Croton Elegies

For Bryan & Mary,
past neighbors, still friends,
Helen Bardini

Essential Poets Series 45

Antonio Barolini

Croton Elegies

*Translated from the Italian
by Helen Barolini*

With a Preface by Luigi Barzini

Guernica

Montreal, 1991

Original Title:
Elegie di Croton

Copyright © 1991 Helen Barolini.
Translation © 1991 Guernica Editions Inc. and Helen Barolini.
All rights reserved.
Printed in Canada.

The original work was published in 1959
by Feltrinelli Editore (Milano, Italy).

Antonio D'Alfonso, publisher and editor
Guernica Editions Inc.
P.O. Box 633, Station N.D.G.
Montreal (Quebec), Canada H4A 3R1.

The Publisher and the Translator gratefully acknowledge financial assistance from
Il Ministero degli Affari Esteri (Italy) for the translation of these poems.

Legal Deposit - 2nd Quarter
Bibliothèque nationale du Québec and National Library of Canada.

Canadian Cataloguing in Publication Data

Barolini, Antonio, 1910-1971

Croton Elegies
(Essential poets : 45)

Text in English and Italian.
Translation of : Elegies di Croton.

ISBN 0-920717-39-X
I. Barolini, Helen, 1925- . II. Title. III. Series.
PQ4807.A76EA313 1991   851   C91-090025-6

Table of Contents

Preface by Luigi Barzini	7
Il polline / Pollen	14 / 15
L'orizzonte all'West / Western Horizon	16 / 17
La casa / The House	18 / 19
Giorno: il tuo prima e il tuo dopo / Day: Your Before and After	22 / 23
Il tempo necessario / Necessary Time	24 / 25
Il villaggio / The Village	26 / 27
I cimiteri sulle colline / The Graveyards on the Hill	28 / 29
Il peccatore sulla collina / The Sinner on the Hill	32 / 33
Confidenza a Whitman / In Confidence to Whitman	32 / 33
Primavera / Spring	34 / 35
La strada residenziale / Residential Street	36 / 37
Le case fungo / The Mushroom Houses	38 / 39
Canzonetta, a un prete / Lines for a Priest	40 / 41
L'ubriaco canoro / The Singing Drunk	40 / 41
Il primo giorno d'estate / First Day of Summer	42 / 43
Le macchine / Cars	44 / 45
Storia / History	46 / 47
Memorial Day / Memorial Day	48 / 49
Cimitero storico / Historic Cemetery	58 / 49
Elegia d'Europa / European Elegy	50 / 51

Harmon Station / Harmon Station	54 / 55
Momenti del piazzale / Moments in the Station Plaza	58 / 59
Sportello di banca / Bank Teller's Window	62 / 63
Le spose zitelle / Spinster Wives	64 / 65
Biografia / Biography	66 / 67
Dedica / Dedication	68 / 79
Lo straccivendolo / The Junk-Man	70 / 71
Canzoni di emigrante / Songs of an Emigrant	72 / 73
Epigrafe per un suicida / Epitaph for a Suicide	74 / 75
Riferimento letterari / Literary References	76 / 77
La filastrocca del vortice / Lines on a Hectic Life	78 / 79
È forse ipocrisia? / Is It Perhaps Hypocrisy?	80 / 81
I colori dell'Hudson / The Hudson's Colors	82 / 83
L'arabo della benzina / The Gas Station Arab	84 / 85
L'invisibile bufera / Invisible Storm	86 / 87
L'erba falciata / Mown Grass	86 / 87
Musica e ospiti / Music and Guests	88 / 89
Stadium / Stadium	92 / 93
Pallacanestro / Basketball	94 / 95
Apoteosi di Di Maggio / Apotheosis of Di Maggio	96 / 97
Dono delle figlie alla nuova terra / Gift of Daughters to the New Land	96 / 97
Preghiera / Prayer	98 / 99
Commiato / Taking Leave	98 / 99
Biographical Note	101

Preface

Antonio Barolini was born in Vicenza, a *terra ferma* city about forty miles northwest of Venice, where, for some reason, the air is particularly favorable to the hatching of good novelists and poets, who do not resemble each other, to be sure, but all have a common bouquet like the local wines. His grandfather was a sea captain who sailed his own square rigged ship, the three-masted *San Spiridione*. The vanishing memories of the old man's adventures haunted Antonio's youth; he called one of his early books *Viaggio col veliero San Spiridione*. He was probably marked for life by the sailors' curse, the perennial yearning to move on whenever one has been too long in one place and the desire to find a final port and settle down for ever in a solid house which does not pitch and roll, surrounded by trees and birds, from whose windows the view is always more or less the same.

Antonio Barolini wears an amused and patient expression; his small dark eyes sparkle under a wide forehead (the hairline has been receding slowly for years); his shoulders, at fifty-six, have the slight sloop of a watchmaker's or an amanuensis', a man who spends most of his life at a table doing minute and painstaking work. His friends know he is many things all at the same time: a severe intellectual preoccupied with fine ethical and aesthetic points, a religious man, a jolly companion with a witty and biting conversation, and an indulgent man of the world, whom *nihil humanum* can ever frighten or astound. He is perplexed and amused by current morals, for example, but is disinclined to consider them a new and significant dénouement in history, the latest episode in man's glorious struggle against the shackles of prejudice; he suspects them of merely being the contemporary aspect of man's perennial inclination for depravity, decay, and self-indulgence, and of his eternal quest for ennobling justifications for his defects.

It is probably the sailor in him who feels at home in Europe and in America (and presumably in any other continents he would visit), that is, as much at home as a poet can feel anywhere on this earth. His wife Helen and daughters were born in the United States, where he lived eleven years. He has many American friends among his unknown suburban neighbours as well as famous writers and critics. He speaks a foreigner's English and he could possibly have learned to write it, were it not for the fact that Signora Barolini, a writer and poet in her own right, lovingly translated all his work (as she has translated this collection of poems). Some of his best prose has appeared in choice American magazines and his name is well known among literary gourmets. Must we then consider him cosmopolitan? Of course he is cosmopolitan, but not in the obvious American Express connotation of the word. The *vincentino* in him is an indelible coloring underlaying everything and it is perhaps this rigidly provincial quality of his which makes his appeal universal.

This is Barolini, *au fond*, a restless man fascinated by man's capacity to desire one thing and its opposite, the flesh and chastity, wealth and the peace of penury, the life of the spirit and sensual joys, stability and revolution, the roaring loneliness of the modern world and the *gemütlich* boredom of ancient middle class family life in the country. Perhaps the best demonstration of his Janus-like nature is his novel *Una lunga pazzia*, one of the best works in contemporary Italian literature, unique of its kind.

This bi-focal point of view, this clarity of vision, this restless rummaging among peacefully accepted facts, this capacity to be provincial and cosmopolitan, all these tendencies have been doubtlessly honed to a fine point by Barolini's American experience. The United States is still, to an Italian's eye, a forbidding Protestant, nordic, scientific, formally law-abiding, vaguely incomprehensible but admirable country where people of other races and religions are hospitably and absent-mindedly accepted but are subjected to a relentless process of digestive assimilation which, in the end, turns them into blank and neuter human beings, no longer what they were but never quite like the prescribed model. A European, in America, is disturbingly forced to consider, sometimes for the very first time, what he really is, what his countrymen are back home and what they turn into, in the new surroundings, at various stages of transformation. The outlandish landscapes, ideals, disturbing habits, the unfamiliar language without which unfamiliar thoughts cannot be defined, the debatable *lieux communs* which everybody seems to accept supinely as divinely revealed dogmas force us to clarify, explain, justify, defend what others seem to be. The debate goes on inescapably day and night, sometimes in an inner monologue, when reading, writing, and tossing in one's bed at night, or in conversation with friends, on trains, in bars, at dinner tables.

It is a notorious fact that many writers, like the wines of Cyprus, improve when travelling. While they endeavour to explain themselves to themselves they also learn to explain themselves to others. Heine and Turgeniev are early examples; Henry James obviously is the most illustrious prototype. James Joyce could probably never have written so clairvoyantly about Dublin in 1904 if he had not travelled in space and time far from his subject. Great Americans of the twenties acquired their sharp view of the Midwest and their national character in the brasseries of the Left Bank. And so on. Very little has been said of the obverse, the influence of life in America on European writers, possibly because fewer of them crossed the Atlantic in the other direction. And yet an essay could be written on the difference of the work of Thomas Mann or Bertold Brecht before and after their American stay.

All this is disturbing. Nobody likes to vivisect himself, rummage among his insides, draw omens and clues from his own viscera. Nobody likes to question the solid foundations of his beliefs, also because, in the end, one is inevitably led to mend some of his ways. Barolini, too, is clearly not the man he was when he left Vicenza. He has acquired a perception of the Italian scene and of the Italians' inclinations, limitations, vices and virtues which can only be acquired from a distant vantage point. As he is not particularly interested in writing lengthy erudite essays, most of his discoveries are concealed within the folds of his poems.

He is a deceptively simple poet at first reading. His verses often seem to run as easily as water down an incline, sound as smooth as children's or peasants' or *alpini's* song. This, in the pompous and unbending mandarin Italian of literature, is quite a feat. It is also remarkable because Barolini belongs to the incomprehensible generation, the hermetic and cryptic poets who strove to clothe their concepts in dark clouds. In reality it is what he leaves unsaid, suggests, or implies, the emotions he evokes without visible means, his capacity to arrive almost at the limit of what words can say which make him a real poet. When you read his verses you discover, here and there, revealing insights which suddenly illuminate the immediate landscape like a smoker's match in a garden will illuminate, for a brief instant, a patch of treebark, ghostly flowers, a bottle, an attentive face.

Most of his American discoveries are compressed into this deceptively light volume, *Croton Elegies*. Croton-on-Hudson, New York, is where Barolini lived for ten years and where, for the first time since his childhood, he owned a house. His previous house in Vicenza had been destroyed during the First World War and what was left of it together with the land around it had to be sold by the impoverished family. Barolini says in his poem "The House":

> *Here my hope*
> *flourishes in the shade*
> *of giant maples...*
> *Perhaps because in the good times, trees,*
> *I once trustingly honored you,*
> *you now soothe with deep shade*
> *this exile*
> *from those parks of my youth*
> *blasted by war-fire.*

One is tempted irreverently to build a continued essay-like discourse by means of some ingenious and arbitrary mosaic of Barolini's verses, just as gardeners in Europe diligently compose vast and multicolored designs on flowerbeds. In such a strange and seemingly inhuman place, America, Italy becomes even more endearing in retrospect, not the glorious country of history books and art manuals but the humble, slightly ridiculous country of nostalgic peasants.

And yet America is not entirely what she seems at first: one can detect in her a mysterious motherly attraction for all men; she can disturbingly become one's own mother before one realizes. One discovers she is more easily accepted, understood, and loved by the illiterate immigrants than by poets. Illiterate immigrants are emotionally defenseless. Take the junkman Esposito, who proudly drives his truck in Croton:

> *The garbage truck,*
> *goes from house to house,*
> *up and down Croton-Harmon*

> *to the clatter of metal cans*
> *and dented covers*
> *to dump its delights in the river.*
> *— He's happy*
> *because he has no fate different*
> *from the harmony of created things*
> *and I know from where he comes,*
> *this Esposito, my brother,*
> *with his pride in a truck*
> *and his name on a sign*
> *instead of with donkey, or*
> *with the bundles across his back,*
> *among the voices and alleyways of Marechiaro*
> *and to the shrill cry of shoeshine boys.*

By and by even the erudite Italian from the North slowly discovers his own brotherly liens with the despised *cafoni* of the South in the alien surroundings. In little churches, for instance, where the old peasants keep alive the cult of their ancient saints:

> *A church with altars*
> *named for the household saints,*
> *and I know right away that my*
> *roving Italians are around.*
>
> *Superstition of the lares,*
> *laden with false jewels*
> *and little candles,*
> *despised age-old burdens.*
>
> *And so I will strive*
> *on the sea all my life*
> *weighted down by a crew*
> *that continues to curse.*

The new country somehow finds its way into the poet's warm heart. To begin with, he discovers he is not alone:

all the people around him, the workers, the shopkeepers, the volunteer firemen, the players of the brass band, the gas station attendants, the commuters on the trains as well as the proud middle class owners of the flowered villas and, the forbidding Protestants, all were poor immigrants at one time or another.

> *Roots long and short:*
> *we are all emigrants*
> *and the federal banner holds us together*
> *with stripes of red*
> *and silver stars.*

Perhaps America also finds her way into Barolini's heart (as her women have always done with Italian men) because of her singular beauty. It takes time for an Italian, even from the Venetian hills, to recognize it, but one becomes an addict of wide open vistas, the ageless landscapes practically untouched by man, the immense engineering structures like steel cobwebs, or the colors of the river and the tree. The mighty Hudson

> *Green, serene*
> *almost veiled in bluish silver*
> *and overcast with mist...*
> *And one knows mud and water*
> *have made*
> *the beauty of this world.*

One is tempted, of course, to construct a continuous pedestrian discourse but one should refrain. Let the poet speak with his own voice.

Luigi Barzini
Rome, December 1966.

Il polline

Se un buffo di vento
ti solleva
e ti sostiene lontano
sulle onde dei mari
e ad altre rive ti trasporta,

non essere
sterile petalo
o barbaglio di luce
che si dissolve nell'aria,
ma, come polline, dove cadi
affonda la nuova radice
e cresci nuova speranza
e virgulti e nuove foglie
e il mondo sempre medesimo
contempla intorno e stupendo
e consuma l'agro-dolce
liquore della diletta vita,

cara ebbrezza fino all'estremo.

Pollen

If a gust of wind
catches you up
and bears you
far over sea-waves
to other shores transplanting you,

don't be
sterile petal,
dazzle of light
that dissolves in the air
but, like pollen, where you fall
sink new root...
burgeon hope,
young shoots, new buds,
and consider the world about you:
selfsame, stupendous.
Consume the sharp-sweet
liqueur of delectable life,

sweet drunkeness to the very end.

L'orizzonte all'West

Lassú
il monte digrada sul fiume
largo come un mare;
e ruggini
sono in fila contro la riva
a centinaia
i bastimenti invecchiati.

In basso,
filo luminoso d'acciaio, il ponte
di Tappan Zee chiude le acque.

Lí
una strada si misura
col brivido delle vertebre
sul teso arco
del continente per l'West.

Western Horizon

Upstream
  mountain
    slopes to
sea-broad river;

  and old ships
    by the hundreds
  are rusted line-ups
      off-shore.

            Downstream,
  a gleaming stretch of steel,
    and Tappan Zee bridge
    closes the waters.

        There
    a road is measured
  with the vertebra-quiver
  of an arched bow
      that is the continent
          aiming West.

La casa

Qui la mia speranza
rifiorisce all'ombra
di platani enormi.

Lungo il portico
della grigia casa di stucco,
incombente di colonne
sotto gli sporti
e di grondaie ostruite da foglie
(onde chiassosi
traboccano sui sassi
i frequenti acquazzoni),
io appendo gentilezza
di latine ghirlande
e i cadenti gerani
si sciolgono esangui.

Forse perché, ai bei tempi, alberi, un giorno
vi onorai confidente,
ora d'intensa ombra
mi consolate l'esilio
dai giardini di gioventú,
dilaniati dal fuoco.

Accolgo in me
il vostro respiro
e riposo nel desiderio di nulla:
il solo onesto
per chi è sapiente e pago
del ben corto suo vivere.

Sovente,
rabbuffando le chiome,
sale il vento dalle valli dei fiumi

The House

Here my hope
flourishes in the shade
of giant maples.
Along the porch
of the gray stucco house
weighty with columns,
with leaf-filled gutters
that brim
with frequent rain
and noisily
spill,
   I set out the grace
   of italianate garlands
   and hanging geraniums
   unravel pale bloom.

Perhaps because in the good times, trees,
I once trustingly honored you,
you now soothe with deep shade
this exile
from those parks of my youth
blasted by war-fire.

I receive your breath
and rest, desiring nothing:
the only honesty
for who knows and is content
with life's brief span.

Often,
ruffling through foliage,
the wind rises
from river valleys

che circondano il monte,
e in impetuosi contrasti
si restringe di vortici al tetto.

Cosí
tra venti opposti
e opposte speranze
e stormire di fronde
or dilaniate or serene,

dilaniato e sereno
il giorno si consuma.

that circle our hill,
and in sudden contrasts
swirls about the roof.

Just so,
between contrasting winds
and contrary hopes
and rustling of leaves,
now fierce, now calm

fierce and calm
the day passes.

Giorno: il tuo prima e il tuo dopo

Disturbate il sonno, corvi,
e la tepida quiete dei gerani
che nel portico allevo.

Unico siete frastuono.
Il sole appena irraggia dalle tende
opache e l'ombra preme intorno al letto
e posa dove Elena dorme.
Me stesso ascolto
volgente al chiaro della luce, al gioco
dei riverberi vetri.
Come uno specchio il cielo che intravedo.

Il prima e il dopo della mia vita
vi starà scritto, penso; ma non questa
presente catena. Giorno per giorno
mi è nota. Nodo per nodo battuta.
E mi par serpe che striscia tra gli alberi...

O mia vita, forse alla tua fatica
gracidano gli insolenti,
che già sentono l'estremo languire
e l'effimero ardore
del sangue che mi veste.

Sfuggirà anche all'acuto occhio dei corvi,
l'invisibile di prima
e che sarà dopo:
avventura non scritta.

Day: Your Before and After

You trouble my sleep, crows,
and the quiet of geraniums
I grow on the porch.

Yours is the only racket.
The sun scarcely filters
the opaque drapes,
shadow presses about the bed
and rests where Helen sleeps.
Turned to the clear light, to the play
of reflecting glass,
I listen to myself.
A mirror, the sky I glimpse.

The before and after of my life
will be written there, I think;
but not this present chain.
Day by day
I learn it. Link after link
hammered out.
Like a serpent, sliding through trees...

Oh my life, perhaps it's your weariness
the insolent crows caw at,
sensing already the last languor
and fleeting ardor
of blood that invests me.

Eluding even the crows' sharp eyes
the vanished before
and what will be after:
adventure unwritten.

Il tempo necessario

Nulla di me, invece, se non fosse
vissuto questo giorno di accidente
per qualche mortale stagione.
Se il distorto albero
non avesse aperto fronde
di speranze nel sole e sollevato
al tuo cielo verdi braccia
affannate di luce.

Riposare
in quest'ombra di foglie
che l'autunno consuma.

Essere vuol dire
essere stati consunti.
E vivere
vale morire.
E morire
aver vissuto pienamente il giorno
dall'alba al tramonto e la notte.

Necessary Time

Nothing of me, instead,
if each chance day
were not lived
through its mortal season.
Or, if the gnarled tree
had not opened boughs
of hope to the sunlight
and raised to your sky
green arms
frantic for light.

To rest
in this leafy shade
that autumn consumes.

To be
means to have been consumed.
And to live
is to die.
And to die
to have lived fully the day
from dawn to sunset and night.

Il villaggio

Le chiese, la scuola e la banca,
la strada e il semaforo,
il cimitero in salita
come punto d'arrivo.
Il *carillon* per le ore,
il municipio
e si svolge la vita.

Il ranuncolo, l'erba alta
e qualche papavero sbiadito
sui fossi del posteggio.
Le automobili sui bordi,
come scarabei dalle ali raccolte
sotto i lucidi dorsi versicolori.

Formiche e mosche e api
sciamano, di bottega in bottega,
intorno al giorno operoso.

The Village

The churches, the school and the bank,
streets and traffic light;
the cemetery on the hill
as a point of arrival.
Chimes for the hours,
the town-hall:
life unfolds.

Buttercups, tall weeds,
an occasional daisy
in empty lots.
The cars at street curbs
like beetles with their wings drawn
under shiny multi-colored backs.

Ants and flies and bees,
the villagers swarm from store to store
about the busy day.

I cimiteri sulle colline

Troppo teneri
i tuoi pensieri,
tenera primavera
del consumato ieri.

Quegli che ti guarda, strana,
nella tua luce vana;
accoglie l'ora esausta
dell'imminente sera.

Attende che la frusta
batta sul cavallo,
che terribile scatta
al vento della notte.

(Il gallo già pregusta
l'ora dei tradimenti
e *lo stridor dei denti,*
o pallido momento.)

Illusione, tremore
della tua fronte bianca,
o stanca persuasione
della *perduta gente.*

(Inferno, paradiso:
candido espediente.
Papaveri del campo,
gentile fiordaliso...)
Fatelo confidente,

fatelo riposare
sotto l'ombra degli alberi
quegli che può sostare,

The Graveyards on the Hill

Too tender
your thoughts,
tender spring
of a used-up yesterday.

He who watches you,
strange,
in your unreal light,
welcomes the spent hour
of imminent evening;

awaits the whip
scourging the horse
that frighteningly rears
at the night.

(The cock already tastes
betrayal's hour
and — oh pale moment —
the gnashing of teeth.)

Illusion,
your white brow's tremulous —
oh weary persuasion
of a *lost people*.

(Hell, heaven:
ingenuous expedient.
Poppies of the field,
sweet wild aster...)
Make him trustful,

let him rest
under shade trees

collinette di Croton,
pietre dei cimiteri.

Gloria di bandierine
sui già consunti ieri,
dolci arcüate vette;
quegli che si disfoglia
(terra, fame, doglia),
fatelo trasognare.

O vita senza fiamma,
o desolato amare,
grafita speranza
e gamma dei colori,
stinta memoria, danza,
suono che si dilegua.

Teneri pensieri,
gracili alla battaglia;
bruciati desideri,
cenere della paglia.

Cosí, sui cimiteri,
il denso fumo acre
dell'erba che s'incendia.

Cosí, nel cielo intenso,
il nulla torna immenso
e l'ora acerba.

•

E non si può pensare
a cose piú profonde, Croton,
perché la primavera
del mondo le nasconde.

gentle hills of Croton,
cemetery tombstones.

Glory of little flags
on consumed yesterdays,
gentle, rounded hillocks;
he who is undone
(earth, hunger, pain) —
let him dream on.

Oh life without flame,
oh desolate loving,
stone-inscribed hope
and range of colors,
faded memory, dance
sound that drifts off.

Tender thoughts,
frail for battles...
burnt-out longing,
straw ashes.

Thus, over the graveyard,
sharp, dense smoke
from burning weeds.

Thus, in the vehement sky
nothingness is immense
and the hour unripe.

And one can't think
deeper things, Croton,
because the spring of the world
cloaks them.

Il peccatore sulla collina

Amò piú fanciulli che fanciulle,
nel tempo. Ma la vaghezza
delle vere carezze gli mancò
fino all'ultimo, e fu sete furtiva.

Ora sulla collina riposa.
E nessuno gli chiede piú ragione
degli amori che furono,
e giace e tutto rimane segreto:
la gentilezza, la grazia
e la velata stanchezza
e l'inespressa fino all'estremo
non goduta voluttà matura:
la sola degna del giorno di morte.

Confidenza a Whitman

Castigati amori
pettinano l'ordinato paese
nella disgrazia del non peccare.

Tante sono le facce del diavolo
che i posteri ipocriti
non le conoscono e tremano
e, per un diavolo morto,
trascurano il vivo,
la poesia perenne
e la continua pietà.

The Sinner on the Hill

In his time
he loved young men more than women.
But the joy of full embraces eluded him
to the end, his thirst was furtive.

Now on the hill he reposes.
And no more is asked
of the loves that were.
There he lies and all is mute:
kindness, charm,
silent fatigue;
and, unexpressed to the last,
the untasted ripe pleasure
alone worthy to approach death's day.

In Confidence to Whitman

After a group of church-goers in Trenton, New Jersey protested the naming of a bridge for Walt Whitman because of his homosexual reputation, and their wishes pervailed.

Chaste loves
groom the orderly country
whose misfortune is non-sinning.

So many guises has the devil
that the latter-day hypocrites
don't know them and tremble
and, taken with a dead demon,
overlook life,
everlasting poetry
and compassion unceasing.

Primavera

Quando viene primavera e si esce
sul prato, si rastrellano le foglie
secche e si bruciano in gerle di ferro.
Il fumo sale
lento verso le nuvole del cielo
come se fosse
il lontano sacrificio d'Abele.
La terra s'intenerisce.
L'erba rinasce col fresco tappeto
sotto i piedi
e vai col passo leggero nel ritmo
del nuovo mondo, verso la tua pace.

Spring

When spring comes you go out
to rake up the old, dry leaves
and burn them in iron baskets.
The smoke
goes up
slowly
skyward
like Abel's long-gone sacrifice.
The land turns soft.
Grass grows into a fresh carpet
under all feet
and you go with a light step
in the rhythm
of the new world
towards your peace.

La strada residenziale

Due rosse azalee,
la casa dei Kingston.
Una, ma enorme,
sulla porta dei Farmer.
Un rosso ciliegio,
un pero, un pesco fioriti
nel giardino dei Kiriacenco.
I tulipani di Miss Alvarez,
il bosco dei pini.
Una vasca di pesci rossi,
una gabbia di *parakeets*.
All'angolo opposto,
la magnolia e i gerani
di Mister Palusello elettricista.
Un *garage*,
due *garages*.
Un cane
un'aiuola
il platano.
La casa nuova
a un piano,
a due piani.
Tre piani la casa vecchia
del poeta venuto d'Europa.
Radici lunghe e brevi.
Siamo tutti emigranti,
e la bandiera federale
ci tiene insieme
con striscie rosse
e stelle d'argento.

Residential Street

Two pink azaleas,
the Kingston house.
One, but huge,
at the Farmer doorway.
A red cherry,
a pear, a peach, all flowering
in Kiriachencko's garden.
Tulips for Miss Alvarez,
a strand of pines.
A pool of goldfish,
a cage of parakeets.
At the opposite corner
the magnolia and geraniums
of Mr. Palusello, electrician.
One garage
two garages.
A dog
a flower-bed
the plane tree.
New houses
on one floor,
two floors.
Three floors the old house
of the poet from Europe.
Roots long and short.
We are all emigrants
and the federal banner
holds us together
with stripes of red
and silver stars.

Le case fungo

Chiaro del bosco,
tra le radure,
le case fungo
dai tetti bassi.

Chiuse scatole
delle paure,
pallide muffe,
umidi sassi.

Miche e formiche,
truffe pazienti
sull'avventura
di tutti i giorni:

poveri viaggi,
andare, venire,
calcoli, stenti,
logori ostaggi.

Chiaro del bosco,
svoli d'uccelli:
o luce breve,
o pioggia lenta.

Un acquazzone
che ci dischiude
i freschi ombrelli...
e la tormenta
che li sfilaccia.

Una farfalla,
unica immagine
dell'aria. A galla,
c'illumina la faccia.

The Mushroom Houses

A clearing of trees
and in bare patches
the low-roofed
mushroom houses.

Closed boxes
of fears,
pale moulds,
damp stones.

Scraps and ants,
diligent frauds
overlaying
the daily adventure:

wasting trips
coming, going,
plans, privations
outworn hostages.

A clearing of trees,
flittings of birds;
oh brief light,
slow rain.

A shower reveals to us
the fresh umbrellas...

and the storm
that frays them.

A butterfly,
the air's only image.
Floating,
it lights our faces.

Canzonetta, a un prete

Non abbiamo panni nuovi,
tanto vale portare i vecchi.
Quanto li vàluti sul mercato?
Noi siamo tutt'orecchi.

Le tue mani, come le mie
stanche di fatica,
credono nel valore
della moneta antica.

Prendi la carità
del mio ultimo amore
e mettila nel traffico
delle tue attività.

Resta sempre uno spiraglio
per scappare da solo
e, sciolto dal bagaglio,
abbandonarmi al volo.

L'ubriaco canoro

Sono invasato.
dallo spirito di Dio...

È whisky, quel che ho bevuto, non acqua!

Se tu conoscessi la grazia
di questo momento d'oblio,

non mi porteresti in guardina
a smaltire la pacchia.

Lines for a Priest

We haven't new robes
so we'll just wear the old.
How much are they worth on the market?

Your hands, like mine
tired with toil,
believe in the value
of the old currency.

Take the charity
of my last love
and put it in the traffic
of your undertakings.

There's always an escape hatch
to get away alone
free from burden
free for flight.

The Singing Drunk

*I am drunk
with the spirit of the Lord...*

It's whiskey I drank, not water!

If you knew the grace
of this moment of oblivion,

you wouldn't put me away
to sleep it off.

Il primo giorno d'estate

Il camioncino dei gelati
(la campanella allegra)
passa tra gli alberati
viali residenziali.

I bambini,
che giocano nel prato a perdifiato,
smettono e gli vanno incontro:
i nichelini in mano.

I cani, risvegliati,
abbaiano per chiasso
e gli uccelli cinguettano tra i rami.
Si dondolano, frullano
in alto e in basso.

Una cicala urla
nell'ora meridiana:
è la prima di un'estate
di tenere piogge,
che pareva una burla.

È scoppiata e si sente
l'avvenuto momento
da come il cielo vibra
sull'erba radente.

Ogni cosa, nella luce,
ha la trasparenza dell'aria.
C'è un paese al mondo,
dove non sia questa festa?

First Day of Summer

The Ice Cream Man's truck
moves with festive bell
down the treed
residential streets.

Children,
playing with all their might,
break off to go and meet him,
nickels in hand.

Dogs wake and bark,
and birds bobbing,
darting,
chirp among branches.

A cicada thrums
in the meridian hour:
so begins a summer
of gentle rains
that seemed a joke at first.

Now it's burst open and you feel
the ripe moment
in how the sky quivers
over mown grass.

Everything, in such light,
has airy transparency...
is there place in all the world
where there isn't this festival?

Le macchine

Una Ford,
una Chevrolet,
una Mercury,
una Chrysler,
una Lincoln,
una Cadillac
e, se si è re
di qualche cosa,
anche una Rolls Royce.

Ma, per me:
une bicicletta,
una macchina da scrivere,
l'uso di una giardinetta
in Italia e, qui,
di una Chevrolet.

O gaio modo
di essere re.

Cars

A Ford
a Chevrolet,
a Mercury,
a Chrysler,
a Lincoln,
a Cadillac
and, if one is king
of something,
even a Rolls-Royce.

But, for me:
a bicycle,
a typewriter,
the use of a Fiat
in Italy and, here,
a compact.

Oh joyous way
of being king.

Storia

La rivoluzione,
la guerra civile.
(O va
o spacchi.)
L'America fu salva:
rasa
a terra la metà.

Il millenovecentodiciassette,
il quarantuno
e gli attachi dei rossi:
fastidi grossi,
ma fuori di casa.

Ora,
le bandierine sui tumuli
dei veterani
e i cimiteri dei pacifici
morti sulle colline.

Questi furono i guai:
ricordi lontani,
eroismi
diventati felicità.

History

The Revolution,
the Civil War.
Double
or nothing.
America was saved:
half of it
razed to the ground.

Nineteen seventeen,
and forty-one
and the Red attacks:
big deals
but away from home.

Now,
little flags over the veterans'
grave mounds,
and cemeteries on the hills
of the peacable dead.

Those were the brawls:
distant memories,
heroics
become happiness.

Memorial Day

Edera immortale, alloro,
rose per la bellezza:
la retorica vale
se non conta gran che!

Non le fanfare. Le bandiere
o la gloria dei trapassati...
e le divise dei vivi son costose!

Le giacche rosse e ricamate
coi gradi d'oro,
boria del corpo di pompiere!

Cimitero storico

Questo il cimitero dei bianchi
pionieri: inglesi, olandesi, tedeschi.
Irving dorme in cima al colle, tra pietre
annerite e grafite di parole.

*

Ma i negri, gli indiani dove
riposano? E gli irlandesi?
E gli italiani, ultimi giunti
tra i peccatori beoni?

La loro stele è forse scritta
tra la polvere delle strade,
dove si sono svincolate
le infangate generazioni?

Memorial Day

Undying ivy, laurel,
roses for show:
oratory's great
if it doesn't mean much!

Not fanfare... nor flags
nor the glory of the dead —
it's the uniforms of the living
that are costly!

Red jackets festooned
with ranks of gold,
pomp for the volunteer firemen!

Historic Cemetery

This is the graveyard of the white
pioneers: English, Dutch, German.
Irving sleeps on a hilltop with
darkening graffitti on the old stones.

But the blacks, the Indians,
where do they lie? And the Irish?
Or Italians — late-comers
among the wine-drinking sinners?

Is their epitaph perhaps traced
in the dust of roadways
where the spattered descendants
were freed?

Elegia d'Europa

Per une gita dalle colline dell'Hudson ai cimiteri dei veterani e a Staten Island, alla "Casa Museo di Gabribaldi e Meucci."

Italia, drappeggiata e barocca,
che sorge dalla tomba
coi dardi di latta, sfolgoranti
intorno al capo,
e il bagliore seghettato della spada
sui trionfi del "Quarantotto."

Puerile monumento!
Due cannoni, in fronte
alla chiostra dell'Alpe.
La bandiera sul pennone.
E la natia città che s'adagia,
rosata di marmi, nella valle.

Stele di tedeschi ammazzati,
venerabili resti
di un'Europa che fu...

Cosí vi ritrovo
sulle colline dell'Hudson
e nella polvere della pianura bassa,
schiaffeggiata dai venti
a Staten Island.

L'eroe degli eroi,
all'ombra di una casupola
fra gli sterpi del mare,
faceva candeline,

European Elegy

For a trip from the Hudson Hills to the Veterans' Cemetery and to the Garibaldi-Meucci Museum on Staten Island.

>Italy, draped and baroque,
>rises from the tomb
>with tin darts gleaming
>about her head,
>and the flash of a saw-toothed sword
>over the triumphs of 1848.
>
>Childish monument!
>Two cannons in front of
>the circling Alps.
>A flag atop its pole.
>And my native Vicenza,
>unctuous with marble,
>makes herself comfortable in the valley.
>
>Relics of slain Germans,
>the old remains
>of a Europe that was...
>
>And so I refind you
>along the hills of the Hudson
>and in the dust of lowlands
>cuffed by winds
>at Staten Island.
>
>The hero of heroes,
>in the shade of a little house
>among thickets of thornbush,
>made candles

nell'ingrato riposo,
tra sogno e navigare.

La casa or s'inghirlanda
di quercia in mezzo al prato.
A quando a quando,
un latrato di cane piccolino
e un tubio di colombi sulla porta.

Tolgo da una bacheca il primo
citofono di Meucci e ascolto
il respiro degli eroi nel tempo.
O voce del mare nella voluta
di una conchiglia morta!

in the hard repose
between dream and sailing on.

Now the house is enhanced
with an oak on the lawn.
From time to time
a puppy-dog's bark
and cooing of pigeons
at the doorway.

I take from a show-case Meucci's first
telephone and I listen to
the breath of heroes in time.
Oh sea voice in the swirl
of dead shell!

Harmon Station

La stazione è una baracca
fatta di rampe e scale,
e fa ponte sopra la ferrovia
che corre lungo il fiume e le sue cale
livide di carbone e di bitume.

Ha l'aspetto garibaldino
d'un quarantotto baldoria.
È vecchia e provvisoria, monumento
di una gesta eroica: un grigio sempre
fresco tra la battaglia e la vittoria,
un velo argento sopra il tono rosso.

Ma qualsiasi cosa
in questo paese
di secolare gente provvisoria!

Anche la rosa
che nasce e muore
e, di anno in anno, ingrossa le radici
presso la porta
fra la polvere della strada.
(I passeri vi ruzzolano amore,
né, per questo,
le continue automobili li turbano,
qualsiasi cosa accada.)

Anche i treni
con le loro campane sonnolente,
e nuovi e venerandi e lunghi e brevi,
passano sotto gli occhi nell'intreccio
dei binari, e mi sembra di guidarli
con pochi tocchi
di bottoni di lampade e di freni.

Harmon Station

The station is a ramshackle place
made of ramps and stairs,
and it bridges tracks
that run river-long, and
past inlets grayed with coal-dust.

It has a Garibaldi air,
a forty-eighter gaiety.
Old and provisional, momument
of heroic gesture: an always
fresh gray between the battle and victory,
silvery veil above the red tone.

But everything's like that
in this country
of time honored provisional people!

Even the rose that blooms and dies
and, year in year out, thickens its roots
in road dust
near the entrance.
Sparrows amiably frisk about it
untroubled
by the continual cars,
by whatever goes on.

Even the trains,
new or venerable, long and short,
with their somnolent bells
pass under my eyes in an interweaving
of rails, as if I'm steering them
with quick touches
of switches and brakes.

Vanno e vengono
e non hanno principio e fine i numeri
dei loro orari.

Basta un errore per uno sconquasso,
in questo andare e venire!
Ma non càpita mai.

Sostano meno di un attimo, a questa
fermata del paesetto del mondo
dove, tra insegne di bandiere in festa,
ho ancorato le mie sere.

They come, they go
...no start, no end
to the number
of their runs.

One slip-up means a wreck
in all this shuffle!
But it never happens.

They pause less than a second at this
stop for the village
in all the world
where,
amid flying of banners in salute,
I have anchored my nights.

Momenti del piazzale

1

Il piazzale
(e la strada vi cala ripida)
sembra una giostra di automobiline
multicolori: girano
intorno al pennone della bandiera
federale. La gente che vi traffica
fa mostra di divertirsi e di giocare,
ma con compunzione.

Nelle ore del solleone,
quando la giostra sta ferma, un facchino
negro col berretto rosso,
legge il giornale accovacciato in terra.

2

Empire State Restaurant, la taverna,
le pompe di benzina concorrenti,
una ghirlanda
di bandierine verdi che stormiscono
alla brezza del fiume e lo stipato
posteggio degli assenti, che lavorano
a New York.

Non c'è
bestia piú paziente dell'automobile
nell'attendere il padrone:
nel solleone,
nella neve e con la pioggia.

Moments in the Station Plaza

1

The road plunges steeply
to the station plaza,
a carousel of colored
cars: they
circle the flag-pole
where the national emblem flies.
The milling people
make a show of elation
of playing,
but with compunction.

In the noon hours of the dog-days
when the carousel is stilled, a black
porter wearing his redcap
reads the paper squat on the ground.

2

Empire State Restaurant, the diner,
competitors' gas pumps,
a flourish
of little green flags that rustle
in the river breeze; and the packed
parking lot of the absent
who work in New York.

There is no beast
more patient than a car
awaiting his master:
in heat,
in snow and under the rain.

Chi la sfoggia
sa di avere un mulo, un asino,
non una carrozza.
Quel dolce tempo esangue
è svanito nell'aria proletaria!

3

La rivoluzione della steppa
è qui arrivata democratica.

Facendo una strada obliqua, educata,
sembra distratta, ma cammima pratica.

Ogni sera l'alcoolizzato
sale sulla corriera di Ossining
che, mezzo sconquassata,
lo aspetta sull'asfaltato.

Io so,
s'egli fosse al mio paese,
canterebbe *Bandiera rossa*.
Qui si sfoga a bere,
e così affoga
l'eresia della riscossa.

Amarezza delle sue candide sere!

4

Non si può dire cosa sia
l'affanno dei poliziotti
nel momento degli arrivi!

Son come spaventapasseri
con le braccia sempre tese,
o son dei grossi passerotti anch'essi,
abbaruffati
nella polvere dei vivi?

Who flaunts one
knows he has a real mule,
not a carriage.
That faded sweet time
has vanished in proletariat air.

3

The revolution of the steppes
has arrived here democratically.
Cutting an oblique path, well-mannered,
it seems distracted, but knows its way.

Every evening a drunk
climbs on the rickety bus
that waits for him
on the road to Ossining.

I know,
if he were in my country
he'd sing the *Internationale*.
Here he lets go in drink
and so smothers
the heresy of insurrection.
Bitter balm of his innocent nights.

4

It's hard to describe
the policemen's anxiety
at the moment of arrivals.

They're like scarecrows
with their arms always taut;
or are they, too, just some big
sparrows
rumpled
in the dust of the living?

Sportello di banca

Quand'ero scrittore di vaglia, dietro
lo sportello di un ufficio di banca,
avevo sempre a che fare
con la faccia di malumore
di Re Vittorio.

Era cosí brontolone
e mi faceva tanto sospirare,
che avevo finito
col volergli bene,
anche se mi aveva tradito.

Il giovane
che paga la moneta del mio pane
americano, non conosce
la fragile mia storia di poeta.

Malinconico, mi dona
malinconiche facce;
e io non oso consolarlo, in cambio,
con l'allegrezza della mia corona.

Bank Teller's Window

When I was a real writer —
a writer of checks —
and teller behind a bank wicket,
I always had to do
with the cranky face
of King Vittorio.

He was so sour
and he caused me so much trouble
that I ended up
liking him
even if he did betray me.

The young man,
who counts out the money
for my American bread, doesn't know
my tenuous story as poet.

Glumly he doles out glum faces:
and I dare not console him,
in exchange,
with the jubilation of my crown.

Le spose zitelle

Le spose zitelle
son prerogativa
di questo paese.

Non sono soltanto
di origine inglese,
ma tutte le razze
che qui sono vive.

*

Le ha toccate l'orgoglio,
stupidità organizzata.
E sono pazze, e la mente fanatica
ne travolge ogni dolcezza d'amore,
catena di vanità
e ipocrisia democratica.

Spinster Wives

Spinster wives
are a speciality
of this country.

They are not only
of English origin
but of all the races
that thrive here.

*

Pride has touched them,
administrative dullness.
And they're crazy, fanatically
routing any bit of love's
sweetness,
chained by vanity
and democratic pretense.

Biografia

La madre calabrese,
il padre napoletano
erano contadini
di sassi senza terra.

Qui, fa lo spazzino
e segue la carriera:
addetto, capo aggiunto
e forse, principale.

La macchina, la scuola,
la casa, la pensione:
giungerà alla sera
come un albero antico
dalla radice anemica
fattosi robusto.

Il carrozzone delle immondizie
(fra un trambusto di bidoni di latta
e di coperchi rotti)
porta di casa in casa
su e giú per Harmon-Croton
e ne versa al fiume le delizie.

È felice
perché non ha sorte diversa
dall'armonia delle cose create:

une serica neve d'inverno
e fiori d'estate
e prati verdi e l'Hudson,

e la polvere
della Strada Numero Nove
dove
ha scoperto l'America.

Biography

A Calabrian mother,
father from Naples
and they were peasants
of rocks without land.

Here he's a garbage man
embarked on career:
employee, section head
and then maybe boss.

A car, school,
house, a pension;
he will reach old age
like an ancient tree
of stunted root
somehow grown robust.

The garbage truck
goes from house to house
up and down Harmon-Croton
to the clatter of metal cans
and dented covers,
to dump its delights in the river.

He's happy
because he has no fate
different
from the harmony of created things:

a feathery winter snow,
flowers in summer
green lawns
and the Hudson,

and the dust
of Route Number Nine
where
he discovered America.

Dedica

A Rocco Scotellaro
perché poeta morto
della mia gente meridionale;

da parte di uno del nord
che non è rimasto,
non perché avesse le ali randage;

ma perché era scritto ch'egli doveva
inviargli questo saluto
a nome di quelli che sono andati
di là dal mare,
forzati dalla vita di cafone
delle solfare
della gramma pietra del meridione.

Non è che siano cambiati.
Molti son restati cafoni,
ma con moneta buona nelle mani!
Anche ricchi e lontani,
son sempre testoni
a proposito dei fatti
del loro paese:
quello di ieri come di oggi.

O poeta calabrese,
proprio perché li ho qui
tra i piedi, tutti i giorni,
vestiti con le penne di pavone
(e tuttavia li amo, come tu amavi
quelli che son costí);

accogli questa ghirlanda, contadino.
Te la manda
un emigrato cittadino.

Dedication

To Rocco Scotellaro
because he's dead
and he was poet
to my Southern people,
this homage from
one of the North
who did not remain,
not because he had
wings for flight,

but because it was meant
that he should
send greeting in the name of those
who crossed the sea,
driven by the life of *cafone*,
by the sulphur mines
by the pitiless rock of the South.

It is not that they've changed
over here.
Many stayed peasants
but with good money in their hands.
Well off and far away
they're still stubborn
about what goes on
in yesterday's land
as well as today's.

Oh Calabrian poet,
just for having them here
on my hands everyday,
in all their plumage
(yet loving them, as you
loved those over there),
accept this garland, peasant.
It is sent
by a city emigrant.

Lo straccivendolo

Sul camion,
da un filo eretto in arco,
come un trofeo di metalli,
risuonano ferrivecchi
di barattoli e stagni.

Passa lento sotto gli alberi,
tra un pispolio degli uccelli,
in una quieta allegria
di distrutti giocattoli.

Lo straccivendolo d'Europa
qui non va col carretto.
Ma la sua scopa
non è detto
che, anche qui, non sia il pendolo
tra la miseria e la ricchezza,
la gloria e la povertà,
perché passa solenne
con l'amistà degli stracci
ma con le solite penne
di Napoli poveracci.

Io so da che paese
viene Esposito, mio fratello,
la boria del camion
e il nome inscritto in cartello;

anziché col somaro, se non già
col fagotto di croci sulle spalle,
tra voci e vicoli di marechiaro
e le grida acute degli sciuscià.

The Junk-Man

From an arched rod
on the truck
the old iron pots
and tin pans clang
like a trophy of metals.

He passes slowly beneath trees
to a calling of birds
and the happy jingle
of broken toys.

The European junk-man
uses no hand-cart over here.
Because he passes solemnly
in the friendship of rags,
and the usual plumage
of Naples' poor devils,
it does not mean that his broom
isn't pendulant
between misery and riches,
glory and poverty.

I know from where he comes,
this Esposito, my brother,
with his pride in a truck
and his name on a sign;

instead of with donkey or
bundles across his back,
among the voices and alley-ways of Marechiaro
and to the shrill cry of shoeshine boys.

Canzoni di emigrante

1

Se in una chiesa trovi altari
con nomi santi casalinghi,
i miei italiani raminghi
so già che sono lí intorno.

Superstizione dei lari,
cincischiata di falsi
ori e candeline, odiate
disgrazie secolari!

Ma so anche che non si può
togliere la paura
senza perdere la pura
pietà dei nostri peccati.

Perciò con questi amari
figli della mia terra,
accendo la candela
e perdo la mia guerra.

2

Anche se si distanzia
la spiaggia dei miei sogni,
non la toccherò mai senza
la gente della mia infanzia.

E cosí arrancherò
tutta la vita sul mare,
col peso di una ciurma
che séguita a bestemmiare.

Songs of an Emigrant

1

A church with altars
named for the household saints,
and I know right away that
my roving Italians are around.

Superstition of the lares,
laden with false jewels
and little candles, despised
age-old burdens.

And yet I know. You can't
take away fear
without losing pure
compassion for sin.

And so, with these rude
sons of my land,
I light my candle
and lose the war.

2

Even if the shore of my dreams
stretches out in the distance,
I will never touch it without
the people of my youth.

And so I will strive
on the sea all my life
weighted down by a crew
that continues to curse.

Epigrafe per un suicida

Basilio Centurione,
italiano, arricchito
per paura della miseria,

quando fu raggiunto
da male mortale,
sentí che ancora gli restava
una spaventosa energia,
demonio pagano
del suo meridionale
paese d'origine.

Poiché voleva spenderla
per sfuggire le sue pene,

non si ammazzò
con un qualsiasi colpo di rivoltella,

ma facendo scoppiare
una bomba di dinamite
(come Sansone,
voleva tutto distrutto)

e morí soprattutto con fracasso.

*

Amico,
non valeva la pena
di far tanto sconquasso!

Ricco o no,
forse non eri figlio del paese
dove i morti non hanno misura
e, da secoli silenziosi,

Epitaph for a Suicide

Basilio Centurione,
Italy-born,
become rich out of fear
of poverty,

when overtaken
by mortal sickness,
still felt
in himself
a fearful energy,
the pagan demon
of his southern
birthplace.

Wanting to use it
to escape his pains,

he didn't die
by ordinary gunshot,

but by setting off
a bundle of dynamite
(like Samson, he
destroyed everything)

and he died above all in an uproar.

*

Friend,
it wasn't worth
making such a crash!

Rich or not,
weren't you once a son of Italy
where the dead are without measure
and, for centuries of silence,

son passati per le vie della fame,
a una solare sepoltura?

Dove i tuoi pari, semmai, per morire,
danno il pranzo di Trimalcione?

Riferimenti letterari

Crotone,
dove le avventure di Ascilto
e dell'efèbo Gitone?

Qualcuno onora
da queste parti
l'osceno Iddio?

Quali ghirlande di rose
a Bacco seduttore
e a Venere dea,
nata dalle sponde d'amore?

Come osare,
in questo pulito
villaggio conformista, rammentare
anche il nome dell'invertito Encolpio?

have passed through hunger
to sun-drenched burial?

Where those like you, to die,
put on (if anything)
a Trimalchian banquet?

Literary References

*From Croton-on-Hudson to the Ancient Crotone
of Magna Graecia.*

Croton,
where are the adventures of Ascyltus,
and the youth Giton?

Does anyone in
this place
honor the ribald God?

What wreaths of roses
to Bacchus, seducer,
or to divine Venus
born from the crest of love?

How dare one,
in this clean
conformist village, even call
to mind
the name of the pervert Encolpius?

La filastrocca del vortice

Paese
di lunghe strade
per carrozzoni
di saltimbanchi.

Ovunque uguale
l'avventura dell'irreale
fame dell'oro.

Ogni villaggio o casa,
speranza e ora,
sospiro e morte
simili a Croton.

Dentro i soliti
involucri di *cellophan*,
trascinati dal ritmo
di un continuo *can-can*.

Ogni attimo lavorare.
Un lavoro riposare,
la fatica di procreare.

Il Sabato le spese.
La Domenica del Signore:
non amarlo, non servirlo.
Abitudine delle chiese.

Non c'è sosta,
manca il tempo,
fiumi, incanti,
firmamento.

Sempre un West,

di là dall'West.

Lines on a Hectic Life

Country of long streets
for caravans
of vagabonds.

Everywhere the same
adventure of the unreal
hunger for gold.

Any village or house,
hope and time,
sigh and death
is like Croton.

Within the normal
cellophane wrappings,
borne along by the rhythm
of a continual can-can.

Every moment working —
it's a job to rest,
the weariness of producing.

Then, on Saturday, shopping.

Sunday for the Lord:
not to love nor to serve him.
A habit of churches.

There is no break...
time is lacking
rivers, enchantments,
firmament.

Always a West

beyond the West.

È forse ipocrisia?

È forse ipocrisia,
l'invincibile vocazione
alla perfetta felicità
del paradiso terrestre
da regalare ai viventi?

O simonia
l'offerta a tutte le genti
di un vecchio Dio
su misure *standard*,
stampato dalla pubblicità?

Is it perhaps hypocrisy?

Is it perhaps hypocrisy
that undefeated vocation
to the perfect happiness
of earthly paradise
begueathed on the living?

Or influence-peddling
to offer everyone
an old God
cut to standard size,
stamped with publicity?

I colori dell'Hudson

È verde e sereno,
quasi velato in un azzurro argento
e soffuso di nebbia...
ma fu livido e grigio
e battuto dal vento che mordeva
le sue onde di ghiaccio.

È terso
e, nel sole, le rive splendono
rigogliose di boschi popolati.

Ancora, a notte, vive per le luci:
si fondono nel cielo delle stelle
e il ponte, all'estremo orizzonte, come
una raggera di docile fuoco,
lo divide.

Tale l'Hudson, non appena la strada
s'incurva ripida in discesa
dal sommo di Croton.
Altre volte, è biondo
come una chioma dorata.

E s'intende perché di fango e d'acqua
è creata
la bellezza del mondo.

The Hudson's Colors

Green, serene
almost veiled in blue silver
and overspread with mist...
but livid once and gray
and beaten by wind
biting icy waves.

Polished in the sun,
its banks shine
luxuriant, thick with growth.

Again, at night, it lives by lights:
they merge in the star-sky
and the bridge at the horizon
divides it
like a halo of docile fire.

This is the Hudson, as the road
curves in rapid descent
from Croton's height.

Other times it's tawny
like blonde tresses.
And you know why
the world's beauty
is fashioned
of mud and of water.

L'arabo della benzina

Paese delgi arem
delle scimitarre
dei bordelli
delle chitarre...

Il negro
è un allegro discendente
di schiavi importati dagli spagnoli:
se piange,
bisogna lasciarlo cantare;
non c'è
nient'altro che lo consoli.

Cielo fatto di oglio e benzina,
di bestie che mangiano in fretta
e scappano.

Acqua dell'Hudson, rosea come sabbia.

Fratelli, guidatori
di cammelli in lunga scolta
per le vie del deserto:
qui, i cessi sono puliti,
Coca Cola sul banco aperto.

Bevete Shell
all'oasi secca,
sole e strada della Mecca!

The Gas Station Arab

His country are harems
scimitars
brothels
guitars...

The black is a cheerful
descendent
of imported slaves:
let him sing
there is nothing
else that consoles him.

Sky made of oil and gas,
of beasts that gulp it down
and take off.

Water of the Hudson, tawny as sand.

Brothers, camel drivers
on long watch
through desert ways:
here the toilets are clean,
Coca Cola's in the dispenser.

Drink Shell
at the dry oasis
sun and road for Mecca!

L'invisibile bufera

Nella tersa luce
della tua pace, Croton,
tace
l'invisibile bufera?

O la sua voce
si esprime con i grilli
che riempiono i tranquilli
prati
nell'implacabile ora
della mia ospite sera?

L'erba falciata

Il profumo dell'erba falciata
rende acre il tuo sapore, vita,
e accende sul prato la giovinetta
che trema e, nell'aria d'amore,
apre le braccia
e dischiude la faccia
alla bellezza del rossore.
O colomba di un cielo immacolato.

Invisible Storm

In the clean light
of your peace, Croton,
does an invisible storm
lie silent?

Or is its voice
in the crickets
that fill the peaceable
yards
in the unyielding hour
of my host,
the evening?

Mown Grass

The fragrance of mown grass
gives you a pungent taste, Life,
and stokes the young girl on the lawn
who trembles and, in the aura of love,
opens her arms
and reveals her face
in flushed beauty.
Oh dove of a flawless sky.

Musica e ospiti

Ti ascolto
sotto le foglie,
dall'aperta loggia
che domina la strada,
musica del giorno:

or piana, or complessa,
e il frequente ritorno
del verso di un merlo
affettuoso e beffardo.

L'inverno se n'è andato,
quando l'ansia delle tue chiome
è scoperta,
collina della casa,
e sei deserta e nuda.

L'ospite adesso varca
soglie fiorite di azalee,
e la memoria lo accoglie,
gli dà il benvenuto

vestita
delle gaie voci
delle bambine che giocano
sul velluto dell'erba.

Ascolto i tuoi passi
strepere sui sassi,
genio confidente che sosta appena
e mette la posta sotto la porta,
procaccia del villaggio.
Giungono
i saluti d'Europa.
Ma quali
pensieri conduco
al mio mondo nativo?

Music and Guests

I hear you
beneath leaves,
from the open balcony
that looks to the street,
daytime music:

first plain, then complex,
and frequent repeat
of the blue jay's notes,
affectionate and mocking.

Winter has gone,
when the longing of your trees
is disclosed,
hill on which my house stands,
and you are lonely, bare.

The guest now crosses
thresholds flowered with azaleas
and memory receives him,
gives him welcome

dressed
in the blithe voices
of children playing
on the velveted grass.

I listen to your steps
crunch on the stones,
village postman,
faithful spirit who pauses barely
to slip mail through the door-drop.
Greetings from Europe
arrive.
But what thoughts do I turn
to my native world?

Niente divide
il presente dall'ieri e dal domani.
Son gli stessi fili
che legano gli amici
vicini e lontani,
vita che ride.
Sotto le foglie
vi convoco

e vi ritrovo in questa
intensità di luce matutina,
compagni morti e vivi.

Non velo od ombra
che dia la differenza
tra i due stati.

Unico lo specchio
dove contemplo
il vostro volto e il mio,

e non è vecchio
il porgere d'ognuno,
né l'antico desio:
bellezza, amore.

Cosí
del rosato Pinot la quintessenza.

Toni, Michele, Neri...
Luci, ali, vele distese, fiume...
O immacolato ieri
e gentile bersò!

Assenti
e presenti, voi,
su questi prati,
creature perenni
del musicale giorno,
amati ospiti.

Nothing divides
the present from yesterday, from tomorrow.
They are the same strands
that bind friends
near and far,
life that laughs.
Under the leaves
I call you together

and find you again
in intense morning light,
companions living and dead.

No veil nor shadow
to make different
the two states.

One only the mirror where I contemplate
your appearance and mine,

and no one
is old,
nor the ancient longing:
beauty, love.

Thus,
of the Pinot rosé, the very essence.

Toni, Michele, Neri...
lights, wings, sails unfurled, rivers...
Oh blameless yesterday
and sweet arbor!

Absent
and present, all of you,
on these lawns,
enduring creatures
of the musical day,
loved guests.

Stadium

La *majorette*
con le gambe di nudo argento
e il corpetto chiuso tra due sfilze
di bottoni, la mazza scintillante,
l'aigrette sul berretto.

A passo di marcia, la fanfara
e gli studenti sul cannone d'ottone,
trainato, che spara a salve.

I ginnasti spiccano salti in aria,
come zampilli o delfini
nel miracolo del mare.

Un carro di pompieri rosso-fuoco,
le campane
nichelate sul davanti, le scale,
le pompe arrotolate
sotto i caschi di gomma.

Finalmente gli atleti, tra sferzate
di riflettori
in gara con le ultime vampate
del sole che sta per morire.

Tutti popolo, signori
della televisione e della radio,
sollevati alla luce artificiale
di un podio di cristalli!

Galli dei pollai,
è giunta la prima ora di notte.
Anticipate il grido dell'alba;
vittoria degli eroi.

Stadium

The majorette
with quicksilver legs
and a slim torso shut between
two rows of buttons, shining baton,
plumes on her hat.

A fanfare in marchtime...
students with a towed brass cannon
firing salutes.

Cheer leaders leap in the air
like spurts, or dolphins
in a miracle sea.

A flame red fire-engine:
nickle-plated bells up front,
ladders,
hoses rolled up
under the helmets.

Finally the athletes in the glare
of arc lights
that compete with last bursts
of sunset.

We're the voice of the people, gentlemen
of radio and television,
in your glass enclosure
up there beneath the lights.

Cocks of the walk,
the first hour of night is upon us.
Welcome dawn's clamor—
the heroes' victory.

Pallacanestro

L'intreccio delle braccia
ricama l'aria,
divaria
in salti silenziosi.

Il pavimento
geme

e i passi
son tonfi di sassi in acqua.

Quel negro
scala
tocca,
cala la palla nel segno.

L'applauso scoppia.
Occhi,
sui denti, di fuoco.

Azzurri
e bianchi
i colori del gioco.

Basketball

An interlacing of arms
embroiders the air,
variegates
in quiet leaps.

The floor
groans

and the shots
are plunks of rocks in water.

The Black
climbs up
reaches,
drops the ball over the rim.

Applause explodes.
Above his teeth
his eyes of fire.

Blue
and white
the colors of the game.

Apoteosi di Di Maggio

Fra quanti eroi e ciclopi
con pupille bagnate di luce,
Tigers o *Giants* o in altre squadre
famosi,

    nessuno piú
lancerà la palla
come il grande Di Maggio! Roteava
la clava sotto gli attoniti occhi
della platea che guardava sospesa...

e poi esultante
di sfrenata gioia plebea.

Dono delle figlie alla nuova terra

Tre fanciulle
porto in dono a questi pionieri,
e affido il mio nome di ieri
ai freschi guerrieri di domani.

O mia fede lontana
di una patria di liberi penati
per ogni casa umana!

Apotheosis of Di Maggio

No matter how many future heroes
and cyclops with light-streaming pupils,
Tigers or *Giants* or other
famous teams,

    no one ever again
will hit the ball
like the great Di Maggio! He swung
his bat under the astonished eyes
of the watching stands, suspenseful...

and then exultant
with unleashed plebian joy.

Gift of Daughters to the New Land

Three little girls
I give these pioneers,
and entrust my name of yesteryear
to tomorrow's fresh heroes.

Oh my distant faith
in a country of free Penates
for every human home!

Preghiera

Qui o là, Signore,
non so dove mi dirai di posare.

Ma è tutto un ponte
sopra il mare
e non ci sono due lingue e due isole.

È unica la vita, la parola, la morte.

È unica la voce degli uccelli,
e il gracile cantare
per le tue verdi isole sul mare.

Commiato

Quando la libertà
toccherà
con la fiamma delle sue ali
ogni vivente

e la terra lieviterà
in una immortale umanità
di creature di Dio,

o signora d'ogni luce, bellezza,

donami un serto di fiori
e carezza di musiche
la memoria delle mie parole,

perché la mia fede finalmente
si sarà aperta
alla tua verità.

Prayer

Here or there, Lord,
I don't know where you'll have me rest.

But it's all a bridge
over the sea,
and there are not two tongues, two lands.

Life is one, and speech, and death.

And one the voice of birds
and their sweet song
over your green islands and sea.

Taking Leave

When freedom

touches
every living being
with the flame of its wings

and the land is leavened
with undying bond
of God's creatures,

then, oh lady of every light, beauty,

bestow a wreath of flowers
and caress with music
the memory of my words,

so that my faith is finally
open
to your truth.

Biographical Note

Antonio Barolini (1910-1971) was born in Vicenza, Italy. He lived for several years in the United States while a journalist for *La Stampa* of Turin, and died in Rome, still active and highly regarded in his literary career. As a noted Italian author his work is included in anthologies and is the subject of various studies.

His published work consists of nine volumes of poetry, three novels, a collection of short stories, and a posthumous philosophical study. His novel, L*e notti della paura* was based upon his escape from prison during the Second World War when he was sentenced for his anti-fascist stand as a newspaper editor. His stories, translated by Helen Barolini, appeared for a number of years in T*he New Yorker* magazine.

In 1950 he married American writer, Helen Barolini, with whom he had three daughters.

Barolini's work in both poetry and prose has attracted the attention of such Italian critics and writers as Benedetto Croce, Pietro Pancrazi, Pier Paolo Pasolini, Eugenio Montale and Geno Pampaloni. He was the recipient of the Bagutta Literary Prize in 1960 for his poetry collection, El*egie di Croton*, as well as the Prato Prize in 1969, and was a finalist for the Campiello and Strega prizes.

•

Helen Barolini is a novelist and the translator of Antonio Barolini's fiction, short stories and poetry.

She co-authored with her late husband a volume of poems entitled, *Duet*. She also edited *The Dream Book: An Anthology of Writings by Italian American Women* (Schocken Books, 1985).

By the Same Author

Cinque canti (1932)
Statua ferma (1934)
La gaia gioventú e altri versi agli amici (1938, 1953)
Il meraviglioso giardino (1941, 1964)
Poesie di dolore in morte di Caterina (1942)
Giornate di Stefano (1943)
Viaggio col veliero san Spiridione (1946)
Il veliero sommerso (1949)
Elegie di Croton (1959)
Poesie alla madre (1960)
Una lunga pazzia (1962)
Le notti della paura (1967)
L'ultima contessa di famiglia (1968)
La memoria di Stefano (1970)
Il paradiso che verrà (1972)

English-Language Editions

Our Last Family Countess, and Other Stories (1960)
A Long Madness (1962)

Bilingual Edition

Duet
Poems in English and Italian
with Helen Barolini (1966)

Printed by
Ateliers Graphiques Marc Veilleux Inc.
Cap-Saint-Ignace Qué.
in May 1991